mighty machines
AIRCRAFT

Written by
Chris Oxlade

Illustrated by
Mike Lacey

p

This is a Parragon Book
First published in 2001

Parragon
Queen Street House
4 Queen Street
Bath BA1 1HE, UK

Copyright © Parragon 2001

Produced by

David West ☖ Children's Books
7 Princeton Court
55 Felsham Road
Putney
London SW15 1AZ

British Library Cataloguing-in-Publication Data

A catalogue record for this book is available from
the British Library.

ISBN 0-75254-674-0

Printed in U.A.E

Designers
David West
Aarti Parmar
Illustrator
Mike Lacey
(SGA)
Cartoonist
Peter Wilks
(SGA)
Editor
James Pickering
Consultant
Steve Parker

CONTENTS

4 Who were the first people to fly?

4 Who built a steam plane?

5 Who flew the first gliders?

6 Who made the first aeroplane flight?

7 What is a monoplane?

7 Who was the first to fly across the English Channel?

8 Which airship burst into flames?

8 Who flew the first airship?

9 Are airships used today?

10 Who was the Red Baron?

11 What were barnstormers?

11 Who were the first people to fly across the Atlantic?

12 Who made the first solo flight across the Atlantic?

13 Who was the first to fly across the Pacific?

13 Which woman flew solo from England to Australia?

14 Which plane is also a boat?

15 How fast could seaplanes go?

15 How do planes land on snow?

16 Which planes have a hook?

16 What was a flying fortress?

17 Who attacked out of the Sun?

18 Who invented the jet engine?

19 What was the first jet plane?

19 What was the first jet airliner?

20 Which fighter can swing its wings?

21 Which plane is invisible?

21 Which plane has back-to-front wings?

22 Which is the biggest plane?

22 Which transatlantic airliner has only two engines?

23 Which airliner carries the most people?

24 Which plane travelled at 7,270 kilometres per hour?

24 Which plane had no wings?

25 Which is the fastest jet?

26 Which jet plane can hover?

26 Which planes can take off and land in cities?

27 Which plane can swivel its engines?

28 Why are helicopters used for rescuing people?

28 Who invented the first true helicopter?

29 What is an autogyro?

30 Which aeroplanes have no engines?

30 Who hangs from a glider?

31 Who flies on hot air?

32 Glossary and Index

Who were the first people to fly?

The first people to make a proper flight were two Frenchmen, François Pilâtre de Rozier and the Marquis d'Arlandes. On 21 November, 1783 they flew for 25 minutes over Paris in a hot-air balloon made by the Montgolfier brothers.

Montgolfier balloon

Who built a steam plane?

The first aeroplane to leave the ground was the steam powered Éole. It was built by French aviator Clément Ader, and had bat-like wings. It only flew for about 50 metres in 1890, and could not be steered!

Éole

Who flew the first gliders?

The first person to build and fly gliders was the German engineer Otto Lilienthal. He made hundreds of flights, starting in 1891. Lilienthal launched himself from hills, and hung under his gliders. He was killed in a glider crash in 1896.

Amazing! In the 14th century Chinese merchants launched kites with people tied to them to see if it was windy enough to set sail in their ships. If the kite failed to fly, they stayed in port until another day. This fact was reported by the famous European traveller Marco Polo.

Otto Lilienthal

Is it true?
People flew by flapping their arms.

No. For hundreds of years people attempted to fly by strapping wings to their arms and flapping them. They became known as 'birdmen', and many were injured or killed, after they launched themselves from high buildings or cliffs. For humans, flying like birds is impossible because we do not have shoulder muscles which are strong enough for flapping.

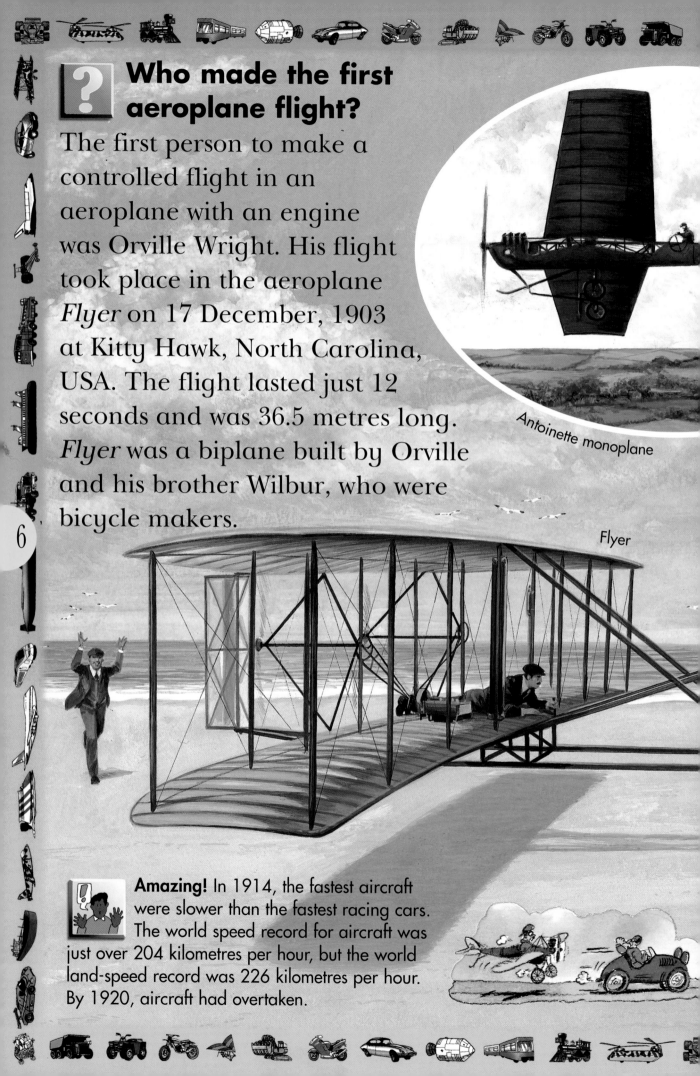

? Who made the first aeroplane flight?

The first person to make a controlled flight in an aeroplane with an engine was Orville Wright. His flight took place in the aeroplane *Flyer* on 17 December, 1903 at Kitty Hawk, North Carolina, USA. The flight lasted just 12 seconds and was 36.5 metres long. *Flyer* was a biplane built by Orville and his brother Wilbur, who were bicycle makers.

Antoinette monoplane

Flyer

6

Amazing! In 1914, the fastest aircraft were slower than the fastest racing cars. The world speed record for aircraft was just over 204 kilometres per hour, but the world land-speed record was 226 kilometres per hour. By 1920, aircraft had overtaken.

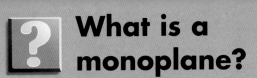

? What is a monoplane?

A monoplane is an aeroplane with one pair of wings. Most early aeroplanes were biplanes, with two sets of wings. The graceful Antoinette VII of 1908 was one of the first monoplanes to fly.

Is it true?
One plane had 20 wings.

Yes. In 1904 Englishman Horatio Phillips built a plane with 20 small wings one above the other. It was a complete failure. In 1907 he built a plane with no less than 200 wings!

Blériot XI

7

? Who was first to fly across the English Channel?

The first cross-channel flight was made by Frenchman Louis Blériot in 1909. He made the trip in one of his own aeroplanes, a Blériot number XI monoplane. It took just 37 minutes to fly from France to England. Blériot won a prize of £1,000.

? Which airship burst into flames?

The hydrogen-filled airship *Hindenburg* exploded in 1937, killing 35 of the 97 people on board. It was one of the two largest airships ever. It was 245 metres long. That's two and a half soccer pitches!

Hindenburg

Giffard's airship

? Who flew the first airship?

Frenchman Henri Giffard flew the first airship in 1852. It had a propeller driven by a small steam engine. Giffard travelled 27 kilometres at 8 kph.

Amazing!

In 1802 Frenchman André Jacques Garnerin jumped from the basket of his hot-air balloon above London. He floated safely down under a parachute. It was the first successful parachute jump.

Is it true?

The first non-stop round-the-world balloon flight was in 1999.

Yes. Bertrand Piccard and Brian Jones flew the Breitling Orbiter 3 from Chateaux D'Oex in Switzerland, and crossed the finishing line in Mauritania 19 days, 21 hours and 55 minutes later. Piccard and Jones finally landed in the Egyptian desert.

Breitling Orbiter

Are airships used today?

Today small airships fly above major sporting events. They carry television cameras to give viewers a bird's eye view of the action. They often have huge advertising displays on their sides.

Who was the Red Baron?

The greatest fighter ace of the First World War, Baron Manfred von Richthofen, was known as the Red Baron. Between 1916 and 1918 he shot down 80 allied aircraft. He got his nickname from the bright red Fokker Dr I triplane he often flew in combat.

The Red Baron's Fokker Dr I triplane

Vickers Vimy

Amazing! Some fighter pilots were not allowed to wear parachutes! During the First World War, the commanders of the British Royal Flying Corps banned pilots, gunners and navigators from carrying parachutes to escape from crippled aircraft.

What were barnstormers?

Is it true?
Pilots shot at their own propellers.

Yes. During the First World War, pilots fired machine guns at their own propellers. To start with, propellers were protected by metal plates. In 1915, a system was invented that made sure that the gun fired only when a propeller blade was not in the way.

Barnstormers were stunt pilots. They toured the USA in the 1920s, performing daredevil flying stunts, such as hanging from their biplanes by their teeth. They also gave rides to the public. Barnstormers got their name by flying very low over farm buildings.

Curtiss JN-4 'Jenny'

Who were the first people to fly across the Atlantic?

The first people to fly non-stop across the Atlantic were Britons Captain John Alcock and Lieutenant Arthur Whitten Brown. They flew in a twin-engined Vickers Vimy bomber, in 1919. It took 16 hours and 17 minutes and ended with a crash into a bog!

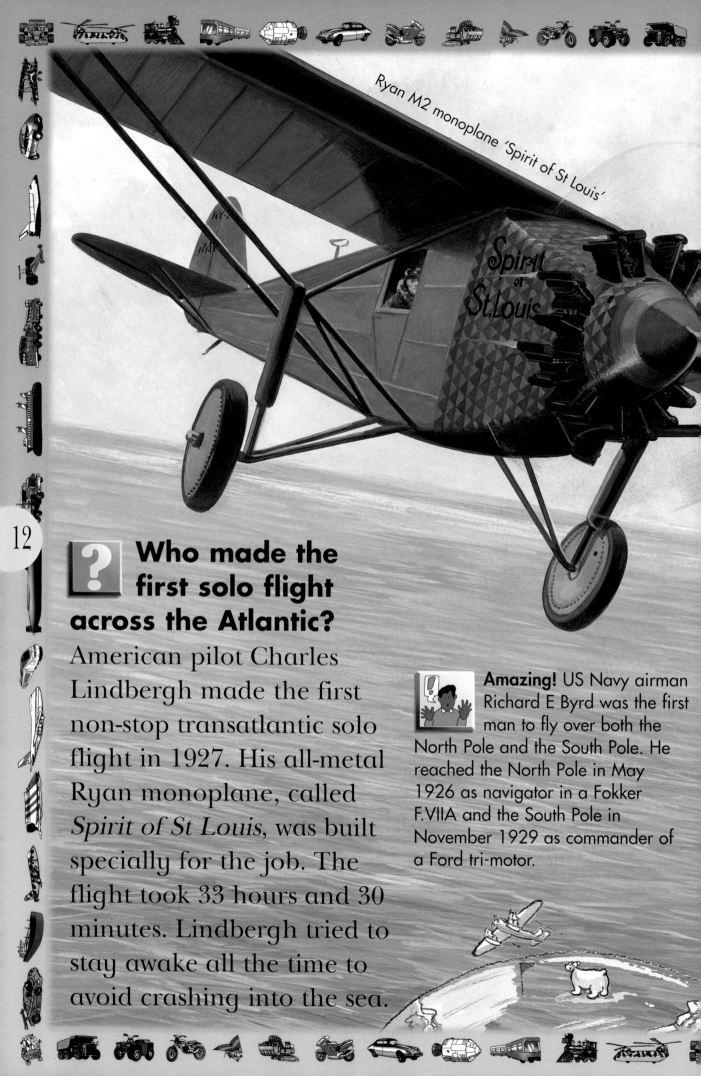

Ryan M2 monoplane 'Spirit of St Louis'

❓ Who made the first solo flight across the Atlantic?

American pilot Charles Lindbergh made the first non-stop transatlantic solo flight in 1927. His all-metal Ryan monoplane, called *Spirit of St Louis*, was built specially for the job. The flight took 33 hours and 30 minutes. Lindbergh tried to stay awake all the time to avoid crashing into the sea.

Amazing! US Navy airman Richard E Byrd was the first man to fly over both the North Pole and the South Pole. He reached the North Pole in May 1926 as navigator in a Fokker F.VIIA and the South Pole in November 1929 as commander of a Ford tri-motor.

Who was first to fly across the Pacific?

In 1928, Australians Charles Kingsford Smith, Charles Ulm and their navigators, made the first flight from America to Australia in a Fokker tri-motor. They refuelled four times on Pacific islands.

Fokker tri-motor

SOUTHERN CROSS

Is it true?
The first solo aeroplane flight around the world took nearly eight days.

Yes. The first round-the-world solo flight was made between 15 and 22 July, 1933. Total flying time was 7 days, 18 hours and 49 minutes for the 25,099 kilometres. The pilot was an American called Wiley Post, and his aircraft was a Lockheed Vega.

13

Which woman flew solo from England to Australia?

English pilot Amy Johnson made the first solo England-Australia flight by a woman, in a Gypsy Moth biplane in 1930. She had many near disasters on the way, including almost flying into a mountain side.

G·AAAH

Gypsy Moth

Amy Johnson

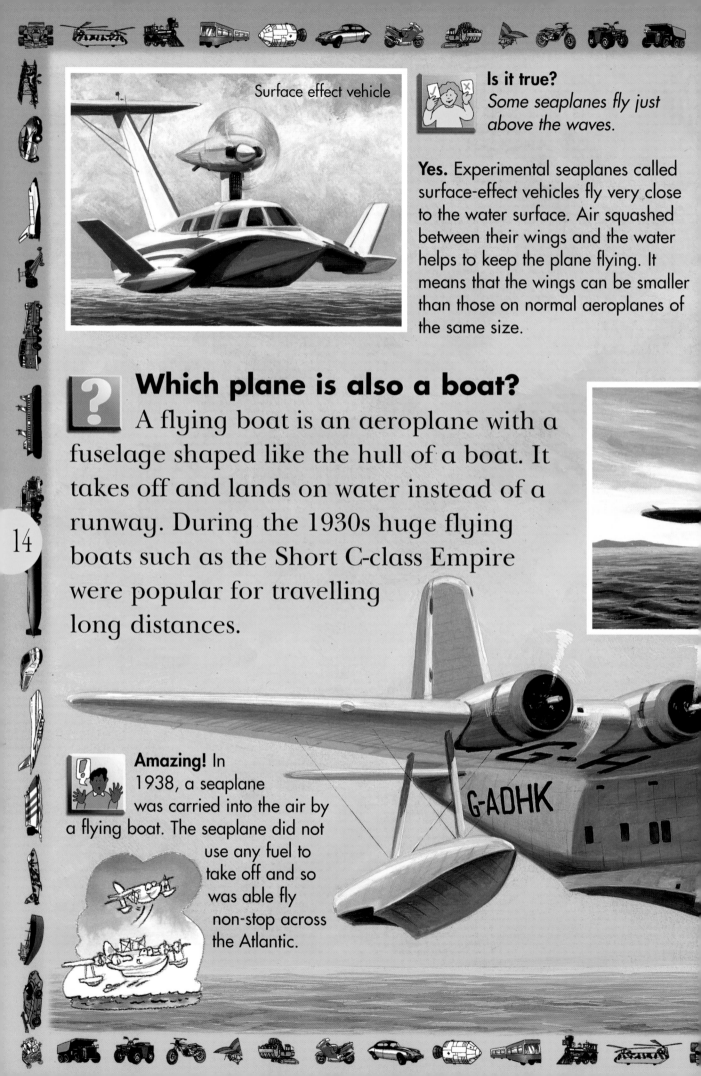

Surface effect vehicle

Is it true?
Some seaplanes fly just above the waves.

Yes. Experimental seaplanes called surface-effect vehicles fly very close to the water surface. Air squashed between their wings and the water helps to keep the plane flying. It means that the wings can be smaller than those on normal aeroplanes of the same size.

? Which plane is also a boat?

A flying boat is an aeroplane with a fuselage shaped like the hull of a boat. It takes off and lands on water instead of a runway. During the 1930s huge flying boats such as the Short C-class Empire were popular for travelling long distances.

Amazing! In 1938, a seaplane was carried into the air by a flying boat. The seaplane did not use any fuel to take off and so was able fly non-stop across the Atlantic.

G-ADHK

? How fast could seaplanes go?

In 1931, a Supermarine seaplane set a new world speed record, and won the Schneider Trophy. It was powered by a special Rolls Royce engine, and reached 655 kph!

Supermarine S.6B

? How do planes land on snow?

Aeroplanes can land on a flat stretch of snow or ice if they change their wheeled undercarriage for skis. One of the first planes with skis was a Fokker F.VIIA used to fly over the North Pole. Modern ski planes take supplies to polar bases.

Short 'Maia' flying boat

? Which planes have a hook?

Planes that land on aircraft carriers have a hook which drops down from the tail on landing. The hook drags along the runway, catches wires stretched across the deck, and the plane stops with a jolt.

Grumman Hellcat

16

? What was a flying fortress?

The Boeing B-17 Flying Fortress was a four-engined heavy bomber flown by the Allies during the Second World War. It had thick armour and four swivelling gun turrets. In all, 12,731 Flying Fortresses were built. between 1935 and 1945.

Flying Fortress

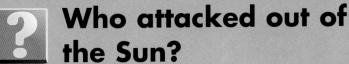

❓ Who attacked out of the Sun?

Second World War Japanese fighter pilots deliberately flew towards their targets from the direction of the Sun. This made it very difficult for enemy pilots and gunners to see the fighters because of the Sun's bright glare in the background.

P-51 Mustang

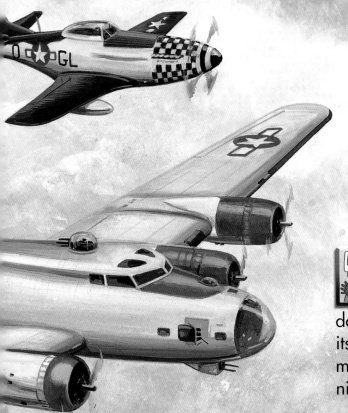

17

Amazing! The Northrop P-61 Black Widow hunted enemy planes at night. It was able to do this because it had a radar system in its nose. It was also painted black, making it very difficult to see in the night sky.

Is it true?
Some planes were made from wood.

Yes. One Second World War bomber, the de Havilland Mosquito, had a wooden frame and plywood on the wing and fuselage. This made the Mosquito very light, cheap to build, and very fast!

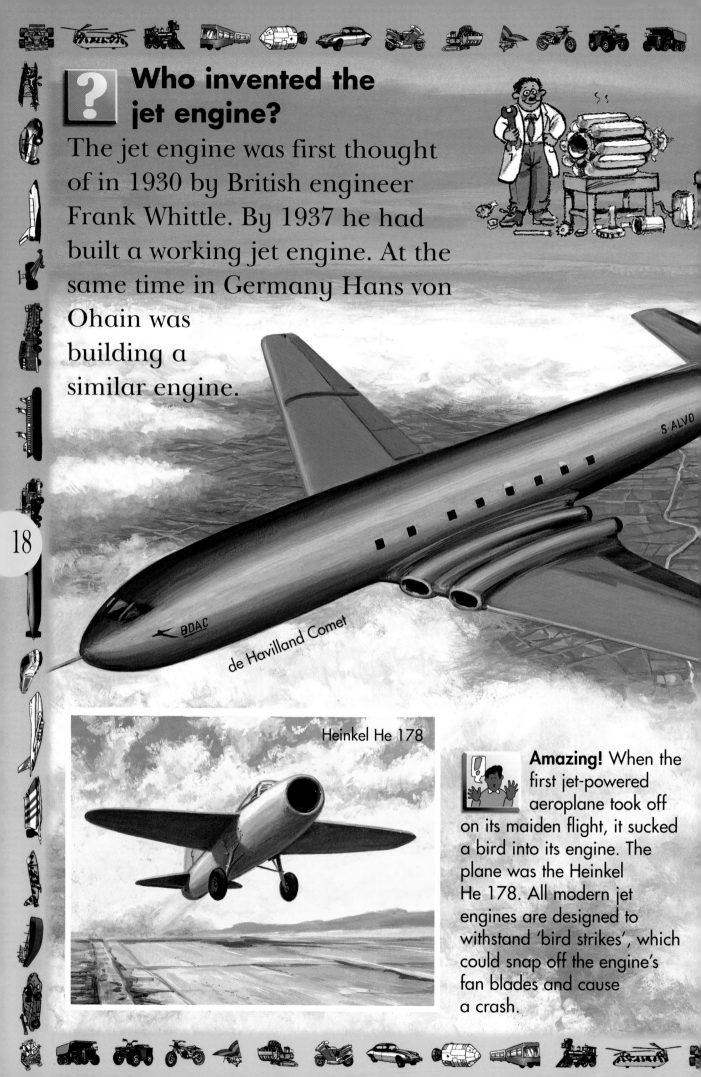

? Who invented the jet engine?

The jet engine was first thought of in 1930 by British engineer Frank Whittle. By 1937 he had built a working jet engine. At the same time in Germany Hans von Ohain was building a similar engine.

S·ALVO

BOAC

de Havilland Comet

Heinkel He 178

Amazing! When the first jet-powered aeroplane took off on its maiden flight, it sucked a bird into its engine. The plane was the Heinkel He 178. All modern jet engines are designed to withstand 'bird strikes', which could snap off the engine's fan blades and cause a crash.

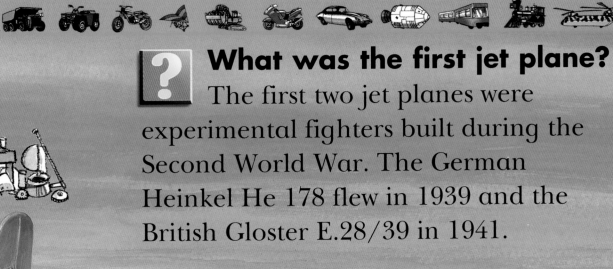

? What was the first jet plane?

The first two jet planes were experimental fighters built during the Second World War. The German Heinkel He 178 flew in 1939 and the British Gloster E.28/39 in 1941.

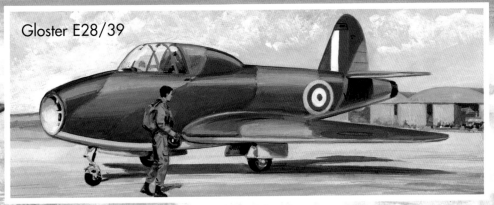

Gloster E28/39

? What was the first jet airliner?

The first jet airliner to carry passengers was the de Havilland Comet I. It had four jet engines set into the wing roots. The first airline service using the Comet was begun in 1952 by the British Overseas Airways Corporation, between London and Johannesburg.

Is it true?
Jet engines have fans.

Yes. At the front of a jet engine there is an enormous fan which sucks in air. Large airliners have jet engines called turbofans, with fans as tall as a person. The fan compresses the air and forces it into the engine. Fuel burns in the air, creating a rush of hot gases which blast out of the engine. They spin a turbine that works the fan.

Air pulled in and compressed by front fans

Exhaust provides thrust

Compressed air and fuel burnt in combustion chamber

19

Is it true?
The first jet-to-jet combat took place during the Second World War.

No. Jet fighters started flying on both sides near the end of the Second World War, but they never met in combat. The first time one jet fighter fought another was in 1950, during the Korean War. A USAF Lockheed F-80C shot down a Chinese MiG-15.

? **Which fighter can swing its wings?**

The Panavia Tornado has 'swing' wings that can pivot backwards and forwards. The forward position is for take-off and landing because it gives plenty of lift when the aeroplane is moving slowly. After take-off the wings are swept back for high-speed flight.

Amazing! Fighter aircraft often fill up their fuel tanks while they are in the air. This is called in-flight refuelling. The fuel comes from a large tanker aircraft. The fighter and tanker pilots have to fly very skilfully to connect up with the fuel hose dangling behind the tanker.

Panavia Tornado

Stealth fighter

? Which plane is invisible?

The Lockheed F117A Stealth fighter is meant to be invisible to radar systems. The F117A's flat surfaces and special paint help to scatter enemy radar signals, making it very difficult to track. But an American Stealth fighter was downed in Yugoslavia in 1999.

? Which plane has back-to-front wings?

It looks as though the wings of the Grumman X-29A have been put on the wrong way round, but they haven't. The X-29A was built as an experiment. Its wings make it so unstable that it can only be flown by computers.

Grumman X-29A

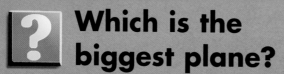

? Which is the biggest plane?

The biggest plane in the world is the six-engined Antonov An-225 transport aeroplane. It can carry other aircraft on its back as well as cargo inside. It can take off weighing a massive 600 tonnes.

Antonov An-225

Boeing 747 'Jumbo Jet'

virgin atlantic

? Which transatlantic airliner has only two engines?

The Boeing 777 flies across the Atlantic with only two engines. Before 1984, all transatlantic airliners had three or four engines in case one failed. Now, engines are more reliable.

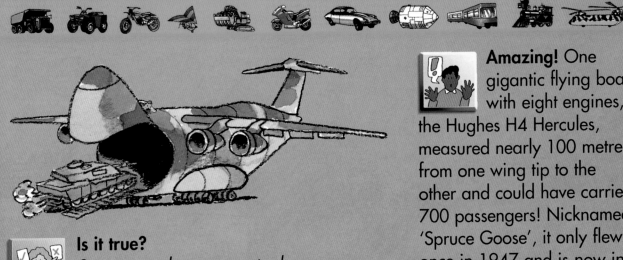

Amazing! One gigantic flying boat with eight engines, the Hughes H4 Hercules, measured nearly 100 metres from one wing tip to the other and could have carried 700 passengers! Nicknamed 'Spruce Goose', it only flew once in 1947 and is now in a museum.

Is it true?
Some aeroplanes carry tanks.

Yes. Monster military transport planes like the Lockheed C5 Galaxy and Antonov An-124 are big enough for tanks. The Galaxy can lift two 50-tonne tanks, which drive in up ramps in the nose or tail.

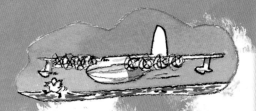

? Which airliner carries the most people?

The airliner that can carry the most passengers is the two-deck Boeing 747 'Jumbo Jet'. Seats for up to 660 passengers can be fitted into the most modern model, the 747-400. There are plans for a double-decker airliner that will carry up to 900 passengers.

Which plane travelled at 7,270 kilometres per hour?

On 3 October, 1967 an American X-15 rocket-powered aeroplane reached 7,270 kph. It's still the world record speed for an aeroplane. The X-15 also holds the altitude record of 107,960 metres. That's nearly 108 kilometres above the Earth's surface!

24

X-15 rocket plane

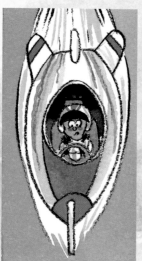

Which plane had no wings?

In the 1970s, US Air Force pilots flew an experimental plane called the X-24A without wings. This rocket plane had a specially shaped fuselage, or lifting body, to keep airborne.

Is it true?
You can travel faster than the speed of sound.

Yes. Some supersonic planes with powerful engines, like Concorde, can fly faster than sound. Sound travels at about 1,225 kph.

Lockheed SR-71A 'Blackbird'

Which is the fastest jet?

The fastest jet aircraft ever was the American Lockheed SR-71A 'Blackbird' spy plane. It holds the official speed record of an incredible 3,529.56 kph, which it set in 1976. In 1974 it set the New York to London record time of 1 hour and 55 minutes.

Amazing! The famous American fighter ace and test pilot Chuck Yeager was the first person to fly faster than the speed of sound (Mach 1). In 1947 he flew the rocket-powered Bell X-1 to Mach 1.015.

Bell X-1

Chuck Yeager

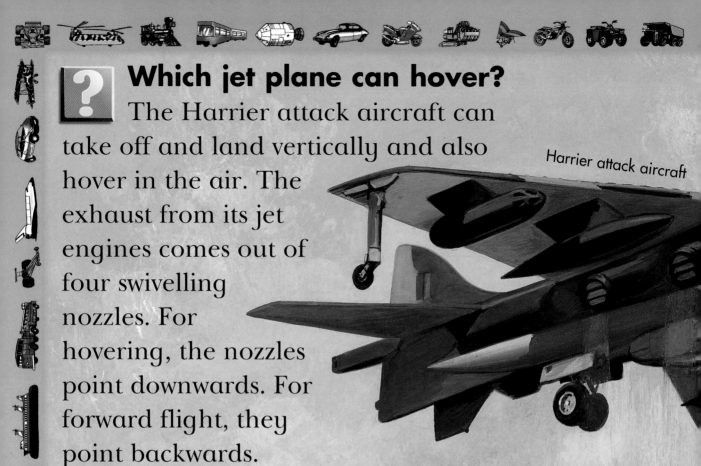

Which jet plane can hover?

The Harrier attack aircraft can take off and land vertically and also hover in the air. The exhaust from its jet engines comes out of four swivelling nozzles. For hovering, the nozzles point downwards. For forward flight, they point backwards.

Harrier attack aircraft

Amazing! Engineers built a bizarre machine nicknamed the 'Flying Bedstead' to test vertical take-off and landing aircraft. It had two jet engines, and its real name was the Thrust Measuring Rig.

de Havilland Dash

Which planes can take off and land in cities?

The de Havilland Dash flies between small airports with short runways that are often near city centres. The Dash can take off and land on a runway only a few hundred metres long.

❓ **Which plane can swivel its engines?**

The Bell/Boeing V-22 Osprey is part helicopter, part aeroplane. It has propellers or proprotors, which swivel upright for take-off, and it works like a helicopter. To go forwards, they swivel down and it flies like a plane.

Bell/Boeing V-22

27

 Is it true?
People can fly with jet-packs.

Yes. By strapping on the Bell rocket belt, a pilot could take off and hover in the air. At the beginning of the film *Thunderball*, James Bond escapes from his enemies with one. However the amount of fuel stored in the rocket belt limits the flying time to less than 30 seconds.

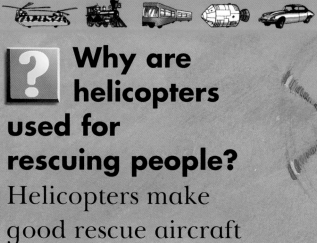

? Why are helicopters used for rescuing people?

Helicopters make good rescue aircraft because they can hover in the air and land in small spaces. At sea they hover while the crew pull people from the water. They are also used to lift injured mountaineers to hospital.

Westland Sea King

Sikorsky VS-300

Amazing! Helicopters can be used as cranes! 'Skycranes' can move heavy objects over short distances. They have a cargo space where the fuselage normally is.

28

? Who invented the first true helicopter?

People had been making brief helicopter flights since 1907, but the first successful helicopter flight was in 1939. Inventor Igor Sikorsky flew his VS-300, which had a single main rotor and a tail rotor. This was the ancestor of all modern helicopters.

RESCUE

Is it true?
All helicopters have two rotors.

No. Very modern helicopters have a tail thruster, instead of a second rotor, but most helicopters do have two rotors. As the engine spins the main rotor one way, it also tries to spin the fuselage the other way. A second rotor on the tail stops this happening. On twin-rotor helicopters, the main rotors spin in opposite directions, so no tail rotor is needed.

? What is an autogyro?

An autogyro has a rotor that is not driven by an engine. As the autogyro is pushed along by its propeller, the rotor spins round automatically, providing the lift that keeps the autogyro in the air.

Autogyro

A-GYRO

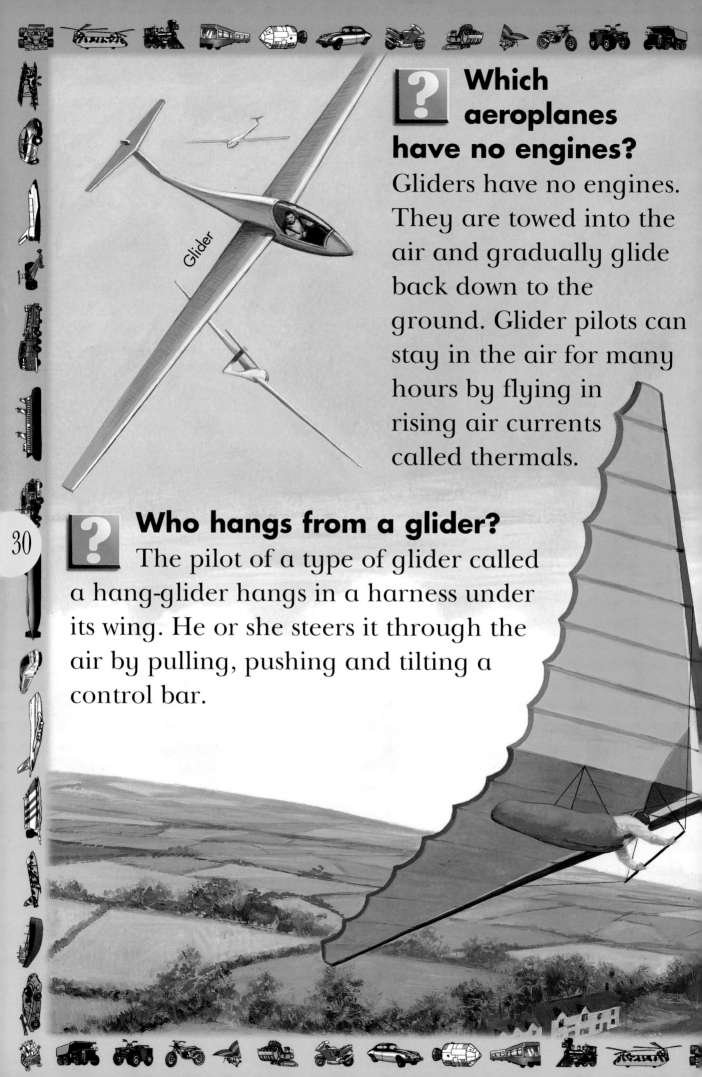

? Which aeroplanes have no engines?

Gliders have no engines. They are towed into the air and gradually glide back down to the ground. Glider pilots can stay in the air for many hours by flying in rising air currents called thermals.

Glider

? Who hangs from a glider?

The pilot of a type of glider called a hang-glider hangs in a harness under its wing. He or she steers it through the air by pulling, pushing and tilting a control bar.

Hot-air balloon

Amazing! Pilots of paragliders can strap tiny engines to their backs to make a tiny plane. A paraglider is a bit like a parachute that fills up with air to make a wing. The pilot hangs in a harness under the wing.

? Who flies on hot air?

Pilots and passengers in hot-air balloons are held up by hot air. A gas burner heats the air inside the balloon, making it hotter and lighter than the colder air outside. This makes the balloon float upwards like an air-filled ball under water.

Is it true?
The space shuttle is a glider.

Yes. The space shuttle is lifted up into space by huge rockets, but lands back on Earth as a glider. The two solid fuel boosters fall away before it returns to Earth, so the pilot only has one chance to get the landing right.

Glossary

Aeroplane An aircraft which uses wings to stay in the air.

Airship A lighter-than-air aircraft with engines to make it move along.

Biplane A small aeroplane with two pairs of wings.

Flying boat An aeroplane with a fuselage shaped like a boat's hull, which can take off and land on water.

Glider An aeroplane without an engine.

Jet engine An engine which pushes an aircaft forwards by burning liquid fuel, and sending a jet of hot gas backwards.

Monoplane An aeroplane with one pair of wings.

Navigator The person in an aircraft who plans the aircraft's route and works out where the aircraft is.

Radar A machine which sends radio waves into the sky and works out where objects are by detecting how the waves bounce back.

Seaplane An aeroplane with floats instead of wheels for its undercarriage, for landing on water.

Solo Alone.

Triplane An aeroplane with three sets of wings.

Undercarriage The lower section of an aeroplane. The undercarriage of most planes is the wheels, but seaplanes have floats, and ski planes land using skis.

Index

Ader, Clement 4
aircraft carriers 16
airships 8
Alcock and Brown 11

barnstormers 11
Blériot, Louis 7
Byrd, Richard E 12

cargo aircraft 22

fighters 20, 21
first flights
  aeroplane 4
  airship 8
  America to Australia 13
  autogyro 29
  controlled 6
  cross-channel 7
  England to Australia 13
  helicopters 28, 29
  manned 4
  non-stop round the world in
  balloon 9

solo round the world 13
solo transatlantic 12
transatlantic 11
  flying boat 14, 23
  Flying Fortress 16

Giffard, Henri 8
gliders 5, 30, 31

hang-glider 30
Harrier attack aircraft 26
helicopters 28, 29
hot-air balloons 4, 9, 30

in-flight refuelling 20

jet aircraft 18, 19
jet engines 19
Johnson, Amy 13

kites 5

Lilienthal, Otto 5
Lindbergh, Charles 12

parachute 9
paraglider 31
Post, Wiley 13

Red Baron 10
rocket planes 24, 25

Schneider Trophy 15
seaplane 14, 15
skis 15
space shuttle 31
Stealth fighter 21
supersonic planes 24, 25
surface-effect vehicle 14
'swing' wings 20

triplane 10

vertical take-off 26, 27
von Richthofen, Manfred 10

Wright brothers 6

Yeager, Chuck 25